BREAKING FREE

Escaping an Exclusivist Christian Group

Breaking Free Publications
Sheridan, California

Breaking Free Ministries
P.O. Box 266
Sheridan, CA 95681

Table of Contents

Introduction

In our ministry we encounter many sincere believers who have a difficult time identifying with and becoming part of local churches. We have discovered that most of these individuals have had a similar type of past spiritual influence. They have been part of, what we deem, "exclusivist" groups. This booklet is a straight-forward look at what identifies a Christian group as exclusivist. Through understanding the nature and workings of these groups, it is our hope that Christians will break free from lingering exclusivist influences.

Before they begin this book, many will assume that it is about obscure Christian sects living in distant mountain communes – some of it might be. As the reader begins reading, however, he may feel we are dangerously close to describing the Baptist or Presbyterian Church down the street – we might be, as well. As will soon become apparent, exclusivist tendencies are not necessarily the result of denominational ties or lack of them. Exclusivist status can simply be a reflection of a group's leaders and the style of ministry they employ. The following outlines identifying characteristics of such groups.

Breaking Free Ministries

WHAT IS AN EXCLUSIVIST GROUP?

A Christian group, local church, or denomination, no matter how orthodox its doctrine, is an a "exclusivist group" if it has the following two characteristics:

- It is divisive towards the rest of the Body of Christ.
- It is excessively controlling of its members.

The following presents these two traits in detail.

Trait #1 – A Christian group qualifies as exclusivist if it is divisive towards the rest of the Body of Christ.

Exclusivism

Common to a Christian exclusivist group is the tendency to separate itself from the rest of the Body of Christ. Groups like this perceive themselves as being *special* in the scope of God's kingdom, perhaps even believing they have an exalted place of ministry in the world and the body of Christ. At the least, they believe that they as a body of people have been bestowed with an extra measure of God's blessing, and therefore glory in their *uniqueness* and feelings of *enlightenment*. Some go as far as to believe that they alone possess the "Truth." They might allow that others have *some* truth, but they perceive themselves as the *most* dedicated, as having the *purest* Truth, the *most* light, or are the most "in-tune" with what God is doing today in the world. Possibly, they see themselves as having truth that has been missing from the Church for centuries – truth they might call the "restored gospel."

Those in leadership may even teach against the pride of *exclusivism*, but will inadvertently foster it by constant references to how "blessed," "enlightened," or "special" the group is. That which they know must not exist in the body of Christ they subconsciously cultivate, because it bears the fruit of great loyalty and commitment in their followers. *(Hearing that you are "special" does feed the ego, and people are drawn to a group or teacher who makes them feel good about themselves.)*

Judgmentalism

Also characterizing exclusivism is *judgementalism*. Christians outside the group are perceived as unenlightened and therefore condescended to as less spiritual. Group members revel with one another in how "enlightened" and "blessed" they are, and take pride in their ability to find fault with those "less enlightened." They delight in pointing out to each other the "absurd" practices and "ridiculous" doctrines held by outsiders. Some will openly laugh and mock at an outsider's "unenlightenment," while others voice their judgments in kind-sounding statements such as, *"Doesn't it just grieve you to see their lack of dedication to God...,"* or *"Isn't it too bad that they are so misled . . ."* The more they judge, the more they reinforce each other in their own superiority. They are severely blind to the spiritual pride that fosters such condescension and judgmentalism. They have fooled themselves by couching their criticisms with humble and compassionate sounding words.

Exclusive groups can usually be divided into one of two camps of "enlightenment" – those who glory in having superior Bible *doctrine* and those who glory in having superior spiritual *experience*s. Some groups have an overlap of both.

In those groups who glory in their "deeper insight" into Bible Truth, pride may drive group members to look for opportunities to show off their knowledge. Not uncommonly, in conversations with Christians outside their group, they will take every opportunity to preach and deliver unsolicited sermonettes. Two-way fellowship or normal conversation with them is very difficult to achieve. Their drive to display knowledge will also involve them in many Bible arguments and debates. For them the Bible is a weapon, but not one simply to be used on the devil and his forces, but one that is used to win battles with other Christians. *(Some may be so taken with themselves and their ability to argue that even after they leave the exclusivist group they will continue to defend doctrines they no longer believe, just because they love to show off their ability to debate.)*

In some groups judgmentalism runs so deep that it is nearly impossible for group members to fellowship with anyone outside their group. They are so convinced of their own superiority and the improbability of finding other true believers, that every other Christian they meet, they automatically judge as a false believer. (Though many won't *admit* to questioning the validity of another's salvation, they may often secretly doubt it.) Upon meeting other professing Christians, rather than accepting them and their testimony of Christ, they will conduct a casual interrogation to identify their error. Once the differences are identified they either end the conversation or engage in debate.

(On the rare occasion that a Christian exclusivist meets a believer outside the group who seems to share or exceed their intense commitment to God, they are amazed and sometimes intimidated. They have come to believe so strongly in their own uniqueness and their own special revelation from God that they find it difficult to believe that others outside their group, or without their doctrine, might also sincerely love and obey God. Inevitably, their pride requires them to find fault with the one who seems so spiritual. They will have to discredit him in some way to maintain the security afforded by their group. One cannot continue comfortably in an exclusivist group unless one can condescend to all those outside.)

There are some exclusive groups whose members do not have the propensity to engage in argument or debate. Those are the groups where *personal* revelation is given equal weight as *biblical* revelation. Their pride will prevent them from "lowering" themselves to argue with anyone about their beliefs or practices. Their confidence in the reliability of their "special revelation," or what they believe to be their "words from God," causes them to patronize and pity others not so enlightened. (It also allows them to escape examining their beliefs in the light of Scripture.)

PRIDE – The root of exclusivism

Pride is the greatest motivating factor in dividing oneself from the rest of the body of Christ. The pride of man loves to find something to glory in. We want to feel special, so we look for something unique about ourselves that will elevate us above all others. Sadly, when our pride is spiritual in nature it is easy to mislabel as *"virtue,"* *"obedience,"* or *"dedication to God."* Many in exclusivist groups become highly sensitive to many areas of sin and purity, but because of the self-deceiving nature of pride, they are completely blind to its presence and its effect upon their lives.

Majoring on the minors

A typical manifestation of the spiritual pride inherent in exclusive groups is the tendency to "major on the minors." They are convinced they have unique insight into God's *priorities*, so glory in both their enlightenment and practice. Although they might hold to doctrines or practices common to orthodox Christianity, the emphasis and importance they place upon those issues becomes a point of division from the rest of the Body of Christ. What the Bible does not portray as a doctrine or practice *central* to the gospel, they give center stage. The over-emphasized issue actually becomes for them a self-validating proof that they are, at the least – *highly enlightened*, or at best – God's *primary* organization. Leaders in these groups persuade the members that a particular issue is a fundamental one and of supreme importance, thereby establishing a standard by which all other groups are judged. If an outside group fails the group's test they are assessed as "carnal" or "apostate," or at the least, unenlightened. **(In some groups, members are warned**

that most if not all outside groups are dangerous and to be avoided.)

For example, a group like this might emphasize something like one's choice of Bible translations. Although some translations are better than others, an exclusivist might believe that to be fully enlightened one must use *only* the translation *he* views as credible. Those who use alternate versions are perceived as wrong in what to him, is a *major* point. Therefore, because they lack his "foundation," anything else they believe, he automatically treats with suspicion or contempt. The problem is not that the exclusivist esteems one translation as best (he might even be correct), but it is the *importance* he places upon it that is out of balance and dangerously divisive.

In the area of *doctrine*, an exclusivist might stress the practice of using the name "Jehovah" in reference to God. Although most of the modern Church accepts the name Jehovah as an acceptable *(though phonetically inaccurate)* transliteration of the divine abbreviation "YHWH," a group priding itself on doing everything "just right" might claim we must use solely this name when referring to God. *They then sight their extended usage of it as* **proof** *that they are* God's most enlightened and most valued organization.

Not uncommonly, groups who glory in particular doctrines preoccupy themselves with those topics frequently in meetings. Over and over, year after year, the same "truths" are hashed out. Biblical proofs and apologetics for their teachings are given time and again, serving to reinforce how right the group is. Every time they hear it all taught, the group nods its head in agreement, then shakes its head in pity for those less enlightened.

Some groups pride themselves less on their doctrinal enlightenment, but rather glory in the "superiority" of their *spiritual experience*. For example, they might acknowledge that other Christian groups "worship" God in song, but they believe that they uniquely see its value to God, so are the only ones giving it the priority God wants for it. Their emphasis upon what they consider to be "proper" worship and praise then becomes for them "proof" that they as an organization are being uniquely led by God. All others not doing it the same are then discredited in their minds.

Letter of the law

Further illustrating this point — those who glory in possessing "accurate" Truth place great importance on keeping what they believe to be the "letter of the law." The problem is that most often what they choose to focus in on are *nonmoral* issues. They tend instead to be issues related to *outward* appearance, *ritual*, or symbolic reverence for God, and not to *true inward purity of heart*.

As an example, the Bible records no name for local assemblies in the early Church. An exclusivist might therefore conclude that to be in God's will, no local church today should have a name. Preoccupying themselves with the *letter* rather than the *spirit* of the law, they project upon God an over-concern about our outside label and packaging, or as Christ put it, "the outside of the cup." Whether you're local fellowship of believers has a name or not, doesn't make you more pure of heart, nor does it make you more acceptable to God. In fact, quite conversely, taking *pride* in whether or not your fellowship has a name makes you more like **Satan**, for *pride* was his downfall.

Some try to justify their emphasis upon "namelessness," citing Paul's admonitions against divisions in 1 Corinthians 3. They claim that naming a local fellowship is divisive to the Body of Christ. This is particularly hypocritical, considering that the Christian groups with names, which the exclusive group accuses of being divisive, are the very ones the **exclusive group** divisively pulls away from. The exclusive groups are divisive by their own choice. Obviously, it is not a *name* that divides – it is *pride*.

It is this misperception of God's values that characterizes much of the exclusivists' belief system, and causes them to make mountains out of molehills. They glory in having every "i" dotted, but pollute with pride anything they do which would otherwise please God. In their intense emphasis on "biblical accuracy" or "true spirituality," they "strain at a gnat and swallow a camel." They strain out small unimportant things having little to do with genuine purity of heart and swallow the camels of pride and self-righteousness. Certainly, God wants for us right doctrine based on accurate biblical knowledge, but that knowledge is useless if it puffs us up, bringing with it division and judgmental attitudes.

The Christian exclusivists are modern-day Pharisees. Many are sincerely zealous for God, but their spiritual zeal is infected with pride. Like the Pharisees of old they seek good feelings about themselves by trying to establish their own worth before God. They may preach vehemently that salvation is by grace, but they subconsciously credit themselves with finding acceptability with God, basing it on their special knowledge, group membership, spiritual experience, or reverence for the things of the Lord. As Paul stated in Romans 10:2-3, *"...they are zealous for God, but their zeal is not based on knowledge. Since they did not know the righteousness that comes from God and sought to establish their own, they did not submit to God's righteousness."* Yes, like a good Christian, a member of an exclusivist group may claim their righteousness is given by Christ, but the presence of pride immediately reveals that they trust in their "self" righteousness – not actually in Christ's *imputed* righteousness.

Wrong concepts of holiness

Often what leads the exclusivist astray is a misunderstanding of the definition of "holiness." They know we are called to be holy, but because they misunderstand what God means by "holy" their consciences become misshapen and they become preoccupied with looking good on the *outside*, neglecting true purity on the *inside*. They value "right-practice" over humility of heart.

Jesus reveals to us what true holiness *is* and *isn't* in Matthew 12:23-28 when He exposed the false holiness of the Pharisees:

"Woe to you, teachers of the law and Pharisees, you hypocrites! You give a tenth of your spices – mint, dill and cummin. But *you have neglected the more important matters of the law – justice, mercy and faithfulness*. You should have practiced the latter, without neglecting the former. You blind guides! You strain out a gnat but swallow a camel. "Woe to you, teachers of the law and Pharisees, you hypocrites! *You clean the **outside** of the cup and dish*, but **inside** they are full of greed and self-indulgence. Blind Pharisee! *First clean the inside of the cup and dish, and then the outside also will be clean.* "Woe to you, teachers of the law and Pharisees, you hypocrites! You are like whitewashed tombs, which *looks beautiful on the outside but on the inside are full of dead men's bones and everything unclean*. In the same way, *on the **outside** you appear to people as righteous but on the **inside** you are full of hypocrisy and wickedness.*

Christ taught that true holiness is not demonstrated primarily by our outward *appearance*, but rather by humility of *heart* characterized by *"justice, mercy and faithfulness."* Outward obedience is absolutely required by Him, but it starts with a pure heart and springs forth from that – *"First clean the inside of the cup and dish, and then the outside also will be clean."* The exclusivist is one whose concept of holiness has to do with maintaining the *appearance* of godliness. He constantly asks himself, "Does *this* 'look' godly?" This brand of *"holiness"* is sometimes referred to as the "religion of the outside." For the Pharisee the *appearance* of holiness **is** in and of itself *holiness* (John 7:24).

An accurate understanding of true holiness is best revealed by its literal meaning. The Greek word for "holy" is *hagios* which means simply, <u>separated</u>. *Hagios* does not carry the idea, as many assume, of having some mystical "specialness" and deserving of "pietistic reverence." In the Old Testament when God told Israel to "hallow" something He was telling them to separate something for special use. The item itself took on no special powers, nor did it become sacred *in-and-of itself.* Rather, it was special only to the degree that it reflected God in some way. Anything hallowed by God was intended to lead us **to** God, deepening our worship of Him and increasing our knowledge of Him. Never was it meant to gain and keep our focus itself.

The people of Israel, much like Christian exclusivists today, misunderstood this concept, so ended up worshipping *things, rites,* and *rituals* as much as, or more than, the One those *things* represented. For example, the Pharisees were offended that Christ healed on the Sabbath, ate with sinners, and didn't perform ceremonial hand-washing before meals. He earned their label of "sinner," because he didn't reverence their traditions the way they did (Luke 7:34).

Not only did Jesus not keep Jewish customs to their satisfaction, but he further offended the Jews when he taught that "inside" sin was equal to "outside" sin, ie: One became guilty of adultery not simply by committing the physical act, but also by simply wishing for the act in the heart (Mat 5:28). He also attributed equal guilt to *hatred* as he did *murder* (Mat 5:21-22). Holiness, he emphasized, was as much an *inside* issue as it was an *outside* one.

In Matthew 12:1-8 Jesus drove home His point when He reminded the Pharisees that King David, when overwhelmed with hunger, entered into the temple area reserved strictly for priests, and ate the "holy" show bread. For anyone other than a priest this was specifically forbidden by God's law, so it should have incurred for David God's wrath. It didn't however, because God was more interested in sustaining David's health than preserving a "tradition." This was particularly convicting for the Pharisees, because they worshipped the *outward form* of the law, missing the real *spirit* of it.

Jesus further exposed the Pharisees' misconceptions of holiness when He reproved them for giving their money to God at the temple, but neglecting their needy parents at home. Jesus asked, *"And why do you* **break the command of God for the sake of your tradition?** *For God said, 'Honor your father and mother'* and *'Anyone who curses his father or mother must be put to death.' But you say that if a man says to his father or mother, 'Whatever help you might otherwise have received from me is a gift devoted to God,' he is not to 'honor his father ' with it. Thus you nullify the word of God for the sake of your tradition.* (Matthew 15:3-6) They let their own parents go hungry in order to keep the letter of the law. All their "rule-keeping" gave them the appearance of "holiness," but reflected no genuine love for God or their neighbor, thereby demonstrating that they had missed what true holiness was.

In the Old Testament whenever God called a "thing" holy he took the risk of people worshipping the "thing" rather than *Him*, and consistently, the worst happened. Time and time again people lost sight of the One who gave the command and worshipped and venerated the "things" God hallowed more than they worshipped God. They, all the while, believed that they were honoring God with their reverence for things. Their proud critical attitudes gave away their ungodliness, however.

God may have told Moses to "take off your shoes you're on holy ground" (Ex 3:5), but it was God's *presence* that made the ground "special," not anything inherent in the ground at the moment of God's presence, nor anything that lingered after He was gone. If for generations to come, Moses' descendants reverenced the place where God spoke to Moses, yet weren't drawn into humility and obedience by their reverence, then they missed the point entirely.

Anytime a *thing* was declared to be special it was only successful if it aimed us back at God – making us love Him more. Traditions and holy things are only valuable if they make us love God and love our neighbor. They cease being useful the moment we use them to fuel our pride. The root of love is humility, so true holiness is impossible without it.

Anyone earnestly desiring to heed God's command to be holy, *"Be holy for I am holy,"* (1 Peter 1:16), will want to know exactly what that means. When we are told to live *holy* lives we are being told to live *separated* lives – lives separated from sin and the self-centeredness that spawns it. When we are *holy* we do not become "sacred," but rather **more** *like Jesus* – reflecting his character. Our holiness is not demonstrated by maintaining pietistic and sanctimonious silence in a church sanctuary during a worship service, or by keeping nonmoral religious traditions, but by having a heart repentant of selfishness, greed, and pride.

If we sacrifice the *spirit of love* for the *letter of the law*, we miss God's point entirely. We've become preoccupied with the "outside" just like the Pharisees. Yes, the outside will reflect what the Holy Spirit is doing on the inside of an individual, but those changes happen from the inside *out* – not the outside *in*. As Paul made it clear to the Church at Corinth, those who appear to be holy on the outside may be devoid of real heart purity. He warned in 1 Corinthians 13:3 that even if we give all our possessions to the poor and our body to be burned, but we lack *love*, it is worth **nothing**.

Simply put, holiness is not demonstrated by a demeanor of reverence, but by living with a pure, humble heart. God is honored by our humility, purity, and love, not by outward forms of piety.

The problem with trying to explain this to a Christian exclusivist is that those who emphasize "piety" are convinced that they honor God by all their "rules of reverence." Their whole life is built on their concepts of "honoring God," so they will resist any attempt to shake their foundation. Often, in fact, that which you might clearly expose to them as a *pharisaistic* rule, regarding a "nonmoral" issue, will be proof to them that you are "carnal" or "unenlightened." They are so steeped in legalism and the false sense of security it brings, that they must first die to their pride before they can genuinely submit themselves to God's grace. Until then they will continue to devote themselves to reverencing the *things* of God rather than striving to reflect the *love* and *character* of God.

Phariseeism

Not only do exclusive groups over-emphasize peripheral Christian doctrines, but most claim special insight and revelation into "deeper" doctrinal truths they believe are unseen and misunderstood by the rest of Christendom. Often these insights regard matters of *sin* and *holiness*. They believe that *they* uniquely understand "true holiness" and therefore are the only ones living lives pleasing to God. The problem is that they define holiness according to their own terms and then hold others accountable to keep their personal standards of holiness. They use not *God's* standards as specifically revealed in the Bible, but their own personal definitions.

True holiness, of course, is something that must be sought by every Christian. In fact, our following of Christ **must** be marked by the forsaking of sin. However, we may define as "sin" for others, only that which the Bible has specifically called sin. We must all be on our guard against concluding that we may hold others accountable to our personal, extra-biblical standards of holiness. Yes, God will convict us that certain things for *us* are sin, but we may not hold others accountable to our personal standards of behavior.

For example, one man might be convinced that for him to wear a mustache hinders his witness for Christ and is therefore not pleasing to God. He consequently, remains clean-shaven believing that a mustache for him is sin. Another man, however, might wear a mustache, having concluded that it helps his witness with the men he works with, and is therefore pleasing to God. Both men have clear consciences before God. Since the Bible doesn't condemn or encourage mustache-wearing, neither man sins. However, neither may use his personal convictions to judge the other. We may hold one another accountable to only those standards of holiness specifically addressed by the Bible, not by our personal conscience, not by what we regard as "deeper insight," and not by what seems to us as reasonable.

We may not use the process of rational deduction to create new sins for modern-day believers. For example, television programming has gotten so corrupt that its influence can be harmful to any viewer – believer and nonbeliever alike. A pastor does well to understand TV's dangers and warn his congregation accordingly. However, that pastor has entered into phariseeism when he pronounces it a *sin* to own a TV. Certainly he would be right to warn his congregation of the danger, and wise to encourage his congregation to keep theirs off, but since God has not specifically called TV ownership "sin" in the Bible, we may not judge TV-owners as sinful. Though 90% of Christians we know may choose not to own or watch a television, *general consensus does not determine what is sinful* – only the <u>Bible</u> does. Wood, plastic, and electronic parts are not materials condemned in the Scriptures – the TV set itself is not "sin." If the Spirit of God convicts an individual that they shouldn't watch TV, then for *them* it would be sin to do otherwise. They may be justifiably concerned for those who watch TV, and would even be responsible to warn them, but they may not hold other believers accountable to the personal standards of their own conscience. The process of rational deduction may be what we use to help us decide how to apply biblical admonitions in our lives, but we have entered into blatant phariseeism when we begin to apply our conclusions to others.

To further illustrate this point, let's consider one more example. In the area of materialism the Bible is overwhelmingly clear: *Don't be materialistic!* (Matt 6:19-20; Col 3:2; 1 John 2:15, 3:17; Eph 5:5) An individual who claims to be a follower of Christ, yet demonstrates the love of money by storing up treasures on earth, and refusing to share with those in need, is certainly living a life contradictory to the gospel. He warrants reproof from the scriptures, and according to 1 Cor 5:11, if unrepentant, he is a candidate for excommunication. From Christ's example of the rich fool in Luke 12:15-21 we can determine that a greedy man is one who amasses wealth and possessions, with no thought to sharing with the needy. However, for those who *do* give to the Lord and who *do* share their possessions with those in need, how can we determine what is too materialistic? What standard does the Bible present to define materialism? Is it up to *us* to decide for others the make and model of car they can drive, or is that between them and God? May we decide for others which new-car features God would consider to be *luxury* and which are *necessary*? Do the Scriptures indicate that a "true" Christian would drive only an *economy* car? By biblical standards do we enter sin to get one with a *sunroof*? Is a VW *godly*, but a top-of-the-line Toyota *sinful*?

When we start to hold others accountable to extra-biblical standards of holiness it becomes our arbitrary decision where we draw the line. Since the Scriptures do not mention Ford, Chevrolet, Toyota, or Audi, we may not make up our own standard of "excess" and hold others accountable to it. Yes, we may be correct in our assessment that someone's choice of vehicle may be a symptom of worldliness, *but we might be wrong*. Judgment on extra-biblical matters is up to God. Where God has not given specific standards, only He may be the judge. To assume that role ourselves is to enter into pure, unadulterated *phariseeism!* We must not fool ourselves – the delight we find in judging others stems not from a pure love for holiness, but strictly from pride.

Pride does not die easy. Once a modern-day Pharisee elevates a secondary issue to a place of importance, it serves as a guide and pacifier for his conscience. With a gratified conscience he feels so good about himself that he will naturally begin to look for other areas of false holiness in which he can glory. Once one has tasted phariseeism, the appetite becomes insatiable. Not uncommonly, Christian exclusivist groups are not just *touched* by phariseeism, but are *rampant* with it. Nonmoral areas preoccupying a Pharisee typically might include: *style of worship, manner of dress, hairstyles, eating of foods, ownership of televisions, dancing, style of music, card-playing, use of spare time, owning of church buildings, reverence for church buildings, proper liturgy*, etc. Though each of these areas merits attention and can relate in some way to morality, they are issues not relevant to salvation and are not doctrines central to the Christian faith. The exclusive group however, focuses great attention on issues like these and others not pertinent to salvation. The attention paid these issues actually serves as the source of pride that divides them from the rest of the Body of Christ.

Feelings of Unity

Often in the Christian exclusivist group, members site as proof of their "divine calling," a strong sense of unity and brotherhood. They are convinced that Jesus' statement that his followers will be known by their love for one another, is fulfilled by the closeness they have to one another. This sense of "closeness" however, is common to *many* groups, and *each* group is convinced that theirs is the only one enjoying what they deem "true love." A study in simple sociology reveals that a feeling of unity and brotherhood is typical of any group with common group goals and an exclusivist mentality. Even in non-Christian, militant political groups personal sacrifice for fellow group members is normal behavior.

Commonly, the sense of unity and brotherhood found in exclusivist groups centers around mutually held values and goals and the concurrent feelings of specialness. Those feelings of specialness and exclusiveness are sufficient to produce a sense of camaraderie. They create a bond between group members similar to that found in a platoon of soldiers on the battlefield. It is an isolationistic "us against them" mentality with the "them" being all those on the outside. In fighting a common adversary, Christian exclusivists find great group strength. The enemy however, ends up being the *Church* – not the devil. Hence, the very thing that produces feelings of unity actually divides the Body of Christ.

There is no doubt that the feelings of unity in an exclusivist group produce acts of love among group members. The quality of this love however, is called into question by the way group members are treated when they decide to leave the group. Often Christian exclusivist groups are famous for shunning and excommunicating those members who leave. Although excommunication is a biblical form of church discipline, Paul was pretty explicit in the types of gross sins warranting such severe action (1 Cor 5:11). Certainly, the desire to fellowship with a different group of believers isn't grounds for withholding love. In fact, Jesus himself taught us that if we only love those who love us we are no better than tax collectors (thieves), because even they do that (Matt 5:46).

Membership for life?

The one characteristic that typifies every Christian exclusivist group is that it is nearly impossible to leave the group without risking rejection and the loss of friendships of those who remain members. Many in exclusivist groups recognize sooner or later that something is wrong with the group and decide to leave. As a result of expressing dissatisfaction with

'God's organization," they are often judged as "rebellious," so find themselves ostracized from those they love. The more extreme groups will actually excommunicate *all* who leave, while the less extreme groups may simply judge and shun only the outspoken ones who depart. Either way, it is very difficult to leave an exclusivist group without becoming alienated from those left behind. This is so, because the nature of exclusivism is *pride*, and the inevitable fruit of pride is *division*.

One of the side effects of belonging to an exclusivist group is that many who leave these groups have difficulty merging into new groups. Their inability to assimilate is not because they are so "discerning," but because they have been trained to mistrust churches, to criticize outside teachers, and to listen through proud, critical ears. It is true that Paul commended the Bereans for their discernment and study of the Scriptures before they accepted his message of Christ, but their scrutiny stemmed from a solid foundation in orthodox Judaism, not from being groomed in pride. Wariness of false teachers is not to be criticized, but wariness resulting from arrogance is.

Integrating into the whole Body of Christ

Certainly, some of the Church today is naive and needs a more sincere desire for Truth and a greater discernment of healthy teaching, but those coming out of Christian exclusivist groups would do well to identify their pride, confess and repent of it, so that they can grow and learn from the Body of Christ. It will be important for them to question not just the doctrine they learned in the past, but especially the *priorities* given those teachings. They must learn that finding *humility* along with holiness in a fellowship is more important than finding agreement with past teachers on peripheral doctrinal issues. Yes, a healthy body of believers must cling to the Scriptures as their only source for divine Truth, but all the truth in the world is useless if it does not lead to humility before God and love for the *whole* Body of Christ (1 Cor 8:1). To get completely free from past influences, and integrate into the Church, exclusivists must remember that much of what they learned was passed on in a spirit of pride.

Finding fellowship in the larger Body of Christ requires trust in God – trust that He has ordained organized local fellowships overseen by elders (Eph 4:11; 1 Tim 3:1; Heb 13:17; Acts 14:23), and trust that He oversees them. Despite the potential for failures and mistakes, God was willing to "risk" the work of His Kingdom with fallible humans. It is to His glory that He accomplishes His plans with weak men who live in bodies of flesh (Rom 7:18-25) and who don't always "get it" quite right (1 Cor 13:12).

God's view of divisiveness:

Often within exclusive groups much is made of the concept of "carnal" Christians. Most outsiders are considered to be less holy & pure and therefore labeled as "carnal" Christians, if they can be called Christians at all. It is interesting to note however, that when the apostle Paul uses the term "carnal" Christian he is describing not believers who continue in open *sin*, but those who are earnest Christians, ones active in the Church, yet who are *divisive* in the body of Christ!

> *"...One of you says, "I follow Paul"; another, "I follow Apollos"; another, "I follow Cephas"; still another, "I follow Christ..." "...Brothers, I could not address you as spiritual but as carnal – mere infants in Christ. I gave you milk, not solid food, for you were not yet ready for it. Indeed, you are still not ready. You are still carnal. For since there is jealousy and quarreling among you, are you not carnal? Are you not acting like mere men? For when one says, "I follow Paul," and another, "I follow Apollos," are you not mere men?*

1 Cor 1:12; 3:1-4

Paul reproved the Corinthian church for their spiritual immaturity, because they acted in pride, claiming allegiance to one leader over another: *"I am of Paul"* and *"I am of Apollos,"* or the most spiritual – *"I am of Christ."* It was **exclusivism** that merited Christians the label "carnal," not lack of "light." Certainly, anyone who professes to belong to Christ, but does not take seriously his call to holiness, would accurately be called "carnal." However, *it is most specifically the ones who claim spiritual superiority and divide themselves from other believers*, which by Paul's definition are not only spiritually immature, but *are in* *sin!* We would do well to learn a lesson from Paul's reproof.

The apostle James, also gave a warning that we should heed. In the 3rd chapter of his epistle, verses 13-18, he warns of pride that leads to divisiveness.

Who is wise and understanding among you? Let him show it by his good life, by deeds done in the humility that comes from wisdom. 14 But if you harbor bitter envy and selfish ambition in your hearts, do not boast about it or deny the truth. 15 Such "wisdom" does not come down from heaven but is earthly, unspiritual, of the devil. 16 For where you have envy and selfish ambition, there you find disorder and every evil practice. 17 But the wisdom that comes from heaven is first of all pure; then peace-loving, considerate, submissive, full of mercy and good fruit, impartial and sincere. 18 Peacemakers who sow in peace raise a harvest of righteousness.

James gives us a standard for determining the source of our "wisdom." He explains how wisdom from above produces *humility*, while carnal wisdom feeds the ego, producing pride with all its fruits. Note that he didn't say it is "knowledge" which produces good or bad fruit, but rather "wisdom." This means that an individual may have accurate "truth," but still lack "wisdom." Missing from their handling of truth is mature, godly discretion rooted in humility.

Paul saw the same danger when he warned in 1 Cor 8:1 that ".. knowledge puffs up, while love builds up." Correct doctrine is important to God. The Bible calls us to pursue accurate knowledge of Him (2 Tim 2:15; Eph 4:13-14), but not for knowledge's sake. The purpose of our pursuit must be to *know* God (John 17:3; Phil 3:10). In knowing God we become like Him, and we will have wisdom from heaven. To have knowledge of God, but to take pride in that knowledge is not to *know* God. If our knowledge is true it is *useless*, for it has done us no good. Correct doctrine is important, but is proven incomplete or inaccurate if it bears the fruit of "exclusiveness." If we are proud of our doctrine then very likely it was passed onto us in a spirit of carnality and pride. Truth is wonderful, but becomes polluted and dangerous when wrapped in pride.

Trait #2 – A Christian group qualifies as an exclusivist group if it is excessively controlling of its members

As should be clear by now, *pride* is at the root of the exclusivist group. The drive to be exclusive stems from an ego that hasn't found security in Christ, so derives it from feelings of superiority and specialness. Pride is ultimately a lack of trust in *God* and a great trust in *self*. Consequently, exclusivist leaders must trust primarily in *themselves* to influence and control the behavior of their group members and not in the Holy Spirit. They establish and maintain this control in several ways.

Leaders control …
1. By establishing the group's authority
2. By establishing their personal authority
3. By personal intimidation
4. By exercising excessive authority
5. By requiring complete conformity of doctrine

1. LEADERS CONTROL BY ESTABLISHING THE GROUP'S AUTHORITY

One of the common means an exclusivist leader uses to gain control is by laying the premise that God works with and puts his hand of blessing on "groups" rather than individuals. This is a powerful form of self-validation, for once the followers accept that it is a "group" that receives God's blessing, and that *that* particular group is the *most* enlightened recipient of God's revelations for the Church, it guarantees that group members will be afraid to leave. They become dependent upon the group and its leaders for guidance and fresh revelation from God. For this to happen, all that is required is that the leaders establish their authority as divinely given. This naturally results in tremendous loyalty from the group followers.

The loyalty, in fact, may be so great that even when group members begin to see inconsistencies, improprieties, or misconduct on the part of the leadership they will frequently not consider leaving, because they have already been convinced there is no where else to go – all other churches and groups have already been discredited. They have heard over and over from group leaders that God is blessing and speaking to *them*. How does one leave the only group that God is with? They couldn't even begin to consider leaving, because they might miss out on what God is doing in the world today. If they went anywhere else they would no longer be on the cutting edge of God's Kingdom. Christian exclusivist leaders maintain strong control over their followers by affirming the belief that God blesses "groups" and that *theirs* is His main group.

It is not uncommon in groups like this to hear not only from the leaders how blessed and enlightened the group is, but also from members. Testimonies reaffirming how wonderful the group is and how this group has changed their life are often given. Though God is generally acknowledged in testimonies, much attention is drawn back to the group itself. Members become elated when group members, who have moved to another city, report back that they just can't find a church or group as good as the exclusivist group, one where the Truth is taught so clearly or the Spirit's power is so manifested. They are so sold on the group that they welcome any news or testimonies that reinforce their devotion.

2. LEADERS CONTROL BY ESTABLISHING THEIR PERSONAL AUTHORITY

It is a natural sociological principle that for a leader to successfully lead, he must gain the trust of those who follow. The more trust he garners the more influence he has. Many successful leaders, both in the secular and religious realm, have gained large followings simply because they exude *credibility*. They communicate and act with such authority that those who want to be led, trust them and are drawn to their leadership. This sociological phenomenon in itself is not evil, but when men "put on" an authoritative appearance it becomes evil. This is often the case with those who lead exclusivist groups. The success of their leadership depends upon their ability to present themselves as having great spiritual authority. The more spiritual authority they are perceived as having, the more credibility they establish in the mind of those who want to be led. The more trust leaders gain, the more influence and control they can exercise.

The more influence they have over their followers, the more they can conform them into what they believe to be God's will. Hence, in order for exclusivist leaders to "lead" (control or manipulate) their followers, they must establish greater and greater spiritual authority. They may attempt to do this in the following ways:

The "Moses Syndrome"

Leaders may attempt to present themselves as having great Bible knowledge, thereby impressing others with their "superior" insights and understanding into deeper biblical Truth. Their knowledge, in fact, may be vast and their doctrines generally sound, but rather than trust the Holy Spirit to bear witness to their authority, they try to establish their own credibility by taking every opportunity to display their knowledge. By their own efforts they gain for themselves more power in people's lives. The problem is not with their *having* great Bible knowledge, for that is a necessity for any good leader. The problem is with their efforts to *display* that knowledge. There is a sea of difference between a man who shares his knowledge strictly for the edification of others and the one who flaunts it for the purpose of impressing them. As we read in Proverbs, a wise man is reluctant to display his knowledge (Prov 12:23; Prov 17:27-28). When he does talk, the wisdom of what he says speaks for itself.

Sometimes, in an effort to feed what some call the "Moses Syndrome" (people's need for strong leadership in their life), leaders learn to speak confidently and in an authoritative fashion. A leader who gives authoritative sounding answers, expressed with confidence, can give great security and comfort to those who don't like to think for themselves, or to those insecure in what they practice. Many people love a "Moses" – a "Papa" who they can look up to and depend on. Many, in fact, who do eventually leave their exclusivist group have grown so dependent on being led by strong leadership that they continue looking for more controlling authority in another exclusivist group. They have cultivated an appetite for *leadership* more than for *healthy Bible teaching*. Once again, it is not the speaking and teaching with confidence and authority that is bad. It is the pretentious flaunting of spirituality, done for the purpose of drawing followers after oneself that is dangerous. For that type of individual it is so important to be seen as knowledgeable, that he will rarely admit ignorance in biblical matters.

New light

One of the attractive things about exclusivist leaders is that what they teach isn't orthodox. Their very appeal is that they speak as if they have keener insights into the Scriptures than all other Bible teachers. Sighting authoritative sounding sources, or with claims of divine inspiration, they convince their followers that they have knowledge of Truths that have been hidden from the Church for the last 2000 years. These new "revelations" are especially attractive to those who are turned-off-by and sit in judgment of the traditional church. They also appeal to the egos of those who want to feel like they are on the inside track among Christians. If a leader can present himself as a teacher with *clever* insights into the Word of God, he can secure followers every time – no matter how heretical his teaching. Christians must be wary of any teacher who claims new insights into the Word of God, or of any who claim to be restoring lost elements of the basic gospel.

But, you may ask, what if Christians have been victims of false teaching and lack proper biblical understanding, shouldn't leaders expose the error and present the Word accurately to them? Yes, people should be taught the gospel accurately, but a teacher serves only to elevate *himself* and appeals to people's egos when he constantly emphasizes that he has special spiritual insights and that the Truth he offers is new and more biblical than what the listener is used to hearing. It is obviously not the insightful teaching of Scripture that is dangerous – it is the teacher's attempts to draw attention to his own authority that is. To have affect on people's hearts Truth doesn't need a teacher to constantly emphasize its uniqueness. True biblical revelation stands on its own authority and the Holy Spirit will always be faithful to bear witness to the Truth.

Hotline to God

Some people are not impressed by Bible knowledge, because they put more trust in spiritual experience. Group leaders of that mind-set, therefore, gain the trust of followers by presenting themselves as having great spiritual "experiences." The greater the experience of the leader, the greater his perceived authority.

Leaders, attempting to establish the significance of their authority, may present themselves as "prophets," causing followers to marvel at their "hotline to God." They give themselves credibility by constantly speaking of their dialogues with God, ie: *"God woke me up at 3:00 this morning and said to me ...,"* or *"The Lord showed me ...,"* or *"The Lord spoke to me yesterday and told me to tell you ..."* With God sighted as the source of most of their ideas and thoughts, it is perceived that the leaders are God's channel for the giving of Truth and direction to the Church. Who would want to ignore the words and disregard the authority of someone who was obviously so close to God!

The Bible, of course, does indicate that God sovereignly leads His people, but the habit of sighting God as the author of all or most of one's thoughts is a highly manipulative technique. It serves only to draw attention back to oneself and enhance one's own authority.

A leader who feels the need to give himself "Moses-like" credibility will soon fall into the *same* trap as Moses – he will be tempted to share in God's glory (Numbers 20). Other than for the purpose of using people's admiration to boost one's ego, the only reason to continually sight *God* as the author of one's words is because one does not genuinely trust in the

Holy Spirit. It is the Holy Spirit's job to bear witness to the Truth. If what is being taught is in line with what God has recorded in the Bible, then the indwelling Spirit can be trusted to enlighten and sanctify the true Believer. A leader's job will be to reaffirm the Bible's authority – not his own.

Those who sight the apostle Paul as their model of "self-credentialing," must be reminded that when Paul offered his divine authority and experiences with God as credentials (2 Cor. 11-12), he was trying to *regain* the trust of a church he himself had planted. With false teachers corrupting the Corinthian Church and challenging his apostolic authority, Paul *reluctantly* boasted of his divine credentials. In his desperation he acknowledged that all his self-credentialing was only an attempt to keep the Church on the path on which he had started them. His motivation wasn't to *gain* followers, but only to *keep* them for the Lord. It was obviously a unique effort by Paul and one engaged in only to solve a crisis. It was also one of an *apostle* – and an apostle whose inspiration from God enabled him to write half of the New Testament. That man who boasts of similar authority today is in a dangerous place, and is certainly not to be followed.

Great spiritual power

Many leaders in exclusivist groups recognize the reverence given to those close to God, so they gladly wear authoritative titles such as "apostle" or "prophet." Many commonly portray themselves as men with a special anointing from God. They may have what seem to be great spiritual gifts and demonstrate what appears to be spectacular spiritual power, but Jesus said that spiritual power is no sign of divine authority. He warned, *"Many will say to me on that day, 'Lord, Lord, did we not prophesy in your name, and in your name drive out demons and perform many miracles?' Then I will tell them plainly, 'I never knew you. Away from me, you evildoers!'* (Matt 7:22-23). Manifestations of spiritual power mean absolutely nothing to Jesus. Words of knowledge, fillings of the Spirit, and scores of decisions for Christ prove nothing about those accomplishing them.

Recent history reveals that Jim Jones, who led nearly 1000 people into mass suicide in 1978, built a large, loyal following because of great miracles he was purported to have done. A documentary film made in the '70's exposed how a fake evangelist named Marjo Gortner preached his way through the Pentecostal circuit, pretending to be a Christian preacher. Marjo, an agnostic, admits people experienced genuine healings under his phony ministry, and he doesn't know how they occurred. Miracles and healing are offered daily by TV evangelists – some have been exposed as frauds, yet even among their staged "miracles" there are documented cases of *real* miracles. The presence of miraculous power in a man's ministry however, is meaningless. Jesus' warning in Matt. 7:21-23 applies to us today.

Countless followers of Christ choose leaders *primarily* on the basis of their spiritual power and the experiences they offer, rather than on, whether or not, what they teach is from the Word of God. Christians lacking a sound doctrinal foundation, and seeking great experience, are easy prey for leaders claiming a special anointing. Anyone who relies on his feelings to direct his devotion is headed for deception.

Experience validates doctrine

For "power" oriented leaders and their followers, "miracles" and "deeper experiences" tend to validate doctrine. They say things like, *"Of course, what he teaches is right! How could one so in touch with God be wrong?"* Though group doctrines may supplement the Bible, experience-seekers readily accept extra-biblical teaching, because they value *experience* more than *Truth!* Sincere believers may, in fact, wrestle with some of the more bizarre teaching of an "anointed" leader, but will ultimately tolerate it and even believe it, because of a leader's apparent anointing from God.

How can you argue with God?

Though rarely claiming infallibility, many exclusivist leaders present themselves as so close to God, and so in-tune with His voice, that followers conclude that to disagree with them would be to argue with *God*. This fear is bolstered by the common exclusivist teaching that we are to "touch not the Lord's anointed." Pretty clever – having God's endorsement makes leaders unaccountable and highly unapproachable. A man gives himself great power to control people if he can convince them he is God's right-hand man.

Judgmental, faultfinding style of teaching

In some groups fellowship is based less on what they stand *for* and more on what they stand *against*. Leaders foster this exclusive mentality in their teaching by constant exposure and criticism of the doctrines and practices of all outside teachers and groups. In fact, in many groups, the thrust of the majority of teaching is *against* something.

The leader whose teaching style is critical and judgmental, not only programs followers to be negative and critical, but effectively bolsters his own personal authority. In his constant criticism of others he impresses his followers with his keen insights into "error" and his ability to point out "false teaching," thereby reinforcing how much "light" *he* has. His followers perceive him as a man of shrewd insight and authority.

Along with helping to establish a leaders' authority in the minds of group members, the tendency to fault-find serves to solidify and reinforce the "specialness" of the group. It galvanizes an "us against them" mentality by fueling group pride. Characteristically, this group-pride causes flock members to emulate the same judgmental attitude as their leaders'. The resulting mocking and belittling of outside groups, their teachings, and practices is the exact opposite of the compassion inherent to the gospel. The spiritually blind deserve our pity and compassion, not our mockery.

Yes, part of instruction in right doctrine requires the exposure of false teaching and the firm confrontation of it, but when we observe error or sin in the life of someone we love, we must not mock and belittle them. Rather, we should respond with genuine loving concern. Only those we hold in contempt do we subject to ridicule. And then, it is only our self-righteousness that delights in pointing out error and will make light of another's unholy or unenlightened state. As Solomon tells us, it is a heart of pride and arrogance that mocks and belittles others (Proverbs 21:24; 11:12).

3. LEADERS CONTROL BY PERSONAL INTIMIDATION

One of the most common ways exclusivist group leaders maintain control of their followers is by **intimidation**. So effective is intimidation as a control technique that exclusivist groups often use it as the primary means of directing and maintaining order within the group. As prevalent it is as a control technique of authoritarianism leadership, rarely is it used consciously or with premeditation. It seems rather to be the expression of the personalities of men who rely upon themselves instead of God to influence and control His sheep.

The symptoms of intimidation within group members are easy to identify. Intimidation is *fear*. When fear fostered by leaders rules your life, you know you are intimidated. It might be fear of what others think of you, fear of what would happen if you left the group, fear of expulsion from the group, or fear for your eternal destiny. If fear is affecting your actions, attitudes, or decision-making ability, then you know you are intimidated, and that someone, very possibly, is using that fear to keep you in line.

Those afraid of how others think of them will have difficulty making decisions for themselves. They feel like they are under constant scrutiny, so weigh out everything they do in terms of, *"What will others think of me? ... What will the leadership say?"* The feeling of being constantly judged creates within them a great *defensiveness*. Those who are severely intimidated are constantly explaining and justifying themselves and their actions, answering imagined judgments before they are spoken. Imagined (and often *real*) judgment can affect everything one thinks, says or does.

The very existence of insecurity in a Christian does not automatically signify that they are under "controlling" leadership. Many people are insecure and defensive long before they ever become part of an exclusivist group. In fact, one of the reasons they might be in the group is because they find security in strong authority. The intimidating authority found in exclusivist groups both appeals to and fosters insecurity.

What makes intimidation work?

In simple terms, to *intimidate* means to make timid; to scare; to inhibit, hamper or hinder; ultimately *to control by fear*. In the exclusivist group *intimidation* is the ability or power of the leaders to manipulate their followers' behavior, thoughts or attitudes by the use of *fear*. For intimidation to "work" requires that the *intimidatee* be afraid – there must be some impending threat. Most often, in the face of strong authority, it is fear of disapproval that rules the intimidatee.

Strong authoritarian leaders have very real power in their followers' lives. They can make life miserable for anyone who does not conform to the group standards, either by public humiliation, levying some action against them, restricting their ministry, or by withholding "fatherly" approval. This threat of misery is a very powerful tool for evoking compliance in group members. Consequently, those wishing to remain in good standing in the group, or those desiring to advance themselves in position must maintain the approval of the leaders. Choosing to stay in the good graces of the leaders then requires that leaders be appeased, hence, the intimidating relationship.

It is important to understand that an exclusivist leader has no power to intimidate by himself – *it must be given him by those who desire his approval*. The strength of his personality, or his high position, may set him up as one that many people will want to be approved by, but he is powerless to intimidate anyone unless they decide they want his approval. A leader only has power to intimidate if he has been given it by followers. The nature of that power is very temporary – he loses it as soon as followers decide they will not seek his approval. This becomes clear when one stops to realize that outsiders are not intimidated or controlled by the exclusivist group leader – he has no power over them because they are not afraid of what he thinks of them. It is only group members who desire his approval, so only **they** fear his authority.

Most people who have been under intimidating authority acknowledge that there are many people in their life who do not intimidate them. This is because they have not given to those particular people that power. We are only afraid of those who can hurt us in some way. And most commonly, it is only those people whose approval we seek who can hurt us.

Never quite approved

For the intimidated follower, approval and affirmation become like the proverbial carrot in front of the horse. Leaders subconsciously dangle it in front of their followers as a means of control – it is offered, but given out in limited doses. One in power who quickly or openly expresses acceptance is not "scary" – few seek his approval or desire it – it is too readily available. Only when acceptance is given out sparingly does it enhance one's power over people. The less approval that is given, the more power one has. Over a period of time, as intimidation increases, a follower's need for approval increases. In extreme situations the follower and their leader develop a "co-dependent" relationship, in which the follower's self esteem actually becomes determined by the leader's opinion of them. If the leader is happy with them they feel good about themselves, but if he is displeased with them, then they feel rotten about themselves. Followers like that ultimately become addicted to their leaders' approval.

The Pharisees are a good example of those who were dependent on others' approval. As leaders they intimidated the Hebrew people into accepting their personal standards of holiness, then flaunted their spirituality to keep the respect they had gained. With fellow leaders they were trapped into trying to "out-spiritualize" one another – they wanted to be *accepted* by their peers, but also to *intimidate* them. Their religious associations created a sort of "mutual intimidation society." This need for approval is called the "fear of man," for which Jesus rebuked them (Matt. 23:25; 6:1-5; Luke 12:4).

Quite naturally, because Jesus did not need the Pharisees' approval he succeeded in intimidating *them.* The Pharisees initially recognized him as someone whose approval would be good to have, because he was popular with the crowds, so they hung around him while he taught and invited him over for meals. When they discovered that they couldn't obtain Christ's approval, and instead found humiliation and rejection, they *despised* him, ultimately plotting his death. Much like with the Pharisees it is not uncommon in an exclusivist group for followers to live in a love-hate relationship with their leaders. They love the leaders when they offer approval, but hate them when they withhold it. Consequently, it is not uncommon in exclusivist groups to find that followers admire and respect their leaders, but grumble and complain about them privately.

Christian exclusivist leaders may maintain their power in people's lives in some of the following ways:

● **Withholding approval** – good behavior or jobs well-done are rarely affirmed; sparingly dispensed compliments tend to keep followers working hard for more; disapproval is communicated by constant scrutiny and criticism, which is demonstrated either verbally or by silent looks of judgment, ie: scowls, shaking of the head, condescendingly rolling the eyes, etc. By not verbally revealing their true feelings towards others, leaders can leave followers feeling insecure in their relationships with them.

● **Public judgment by implication** – criticizing "out-of-line" group members from the pulpit or in front of others without naming names, by sighting them as examples of wrong thinking or bad behavior.

● **Public humiliation** – scolding or reproving fellow adults in public; from the pulpit draw attention to: moms with crying babies, those who leave their seat during a service, sleepers, etc. Potential embarrassment keeps members in line. A senior pastor, by publicly kidding, mocking or belittling his assistant pastor, can intimidate him and simultaneously gain more power by causing group members to disrespect the belittled leader as well. Actually, anyone who appears too capable may be perceived by the leader as a threat and will be kept in place by public humiliation. Leaders may justify their intimidating public rebukes sighting Jesus as their example. Jesus did rebuke publicly, but his targets were generally hypocritical religious leaders. Besides, Gal 6:1 instructs us that our manner in correction of fellow saints is to be humble and gentle. Regular public humiliation is neither.

● **Manipulating with "guilt"** – in personal contacts a leader may take every opportunity to point out followers' failures and mistakes, creating within them a sense of indebtedness. Followers who feel they have let down their leader will be more cooperative, even thankful for their leader's tolerance of them.

● **Condemnation of deserters** – in the more extreme groups leaders speak critically of *all* who leave the group. They don't let anyone think there's ever a pure, God-honoring person who leaves. They teach and threaten that any who leave, or who lose favor with the group leadership, may be on their way to Hell. Leaders create fear with stories of destroyed lives of deserters. In the face of such intense scrutiny, followers are reluctant to leave.

Intimidation by charm & flirtation

One element of intimidation used by some leaders to gain power is *charm and flirtation*. Quite the opposite of the negative control effected by criticism and judgment, a little stroking and flattery on a follower's weak ego can make a leader irresistible. He becomes so good at building his followers' self esteem that they become dependent upon him for good feelings about themselves. They become cooperative group members not because they fear rejection, but because they thrive on being liked. They, like most people, are subconsciously drawn to anyone who can make them feel good.

People like to be liked. They especially like approval from someone important – the more important the person from whom the approval comes – the deeper their sense of well-being. Often group leaders take on a paternal role in their followers' lives – to many they become a sort of "Papa." It is natural to want "Papa's" approval. This paternal appeal however, empowers leaders to manipulate their followers with flattery. Their excessive stroking makes their followers feel "special" and breeds within them an appetite for further approval.

The Bible warns us about those who would manipulate us with charm. Speaking of this type of person in Romans 16:18, Paul says, "For such people are not serving our Lord Christ, but their own appetites. *By smooth talk and flattery they deceive the minds of naive people.*" Solomon warned that "Charm is deceptive" . . . "and a flattering mouth works ruin" (Prov 31:30; 26:28). Paul, in his second letter to Timothy, stated that people will be drawn to teachers who will tickle their ears (2 Tim 4:3). Anyone who seeks to receive from man the security and confidence which we can receive only from a relationship with God has already been led astray. Those who are emotionally lacking are ripe for the charm of a manipulative leader.

The flattery used by leaders may take the form of simple compliments, ie: "That was the best peach cobbler I have ever had, Sister Miller," or, "You do that well, Brother Bob. I wish I had a whole church full of men like you." They may stroke with spiritual praise, ie: "Brother, I believe you are a prophet...," or "You are so sensitive to the Spirit," or "You've got incredible spiritual insight." Like a slick politician, manipulative leaders may flatter a follower by seeking out their opinion on some church matter, thank them for giving it, yet have no intention of using it.

In more experience-oriented groups a leader may draw followers to himself by giving to members personally tailored prophesies, ie: "God has a special plan for you . . . a special ministry, and here it is...," or "Brother So & So, don't leave tonight's meeting yet. God told me He has something special to say to you..." It is highly compelling to hear that a leader, who is so in touch with God, singles you out for special attention.

Some manipulative leaders regularly stroke not an individual's, but a *group's* corporate ego, ie: "You are God's people, the finest people in the world...," or "Brothers and Sisters, you are blessed of God to be so enlightened," or "We are on the cutting edge of what God is doing today," or "Oh, what a wonderful church family this is!"

Before unnecessary fear and suspicion sets in to the reader toward their own pastor, it must be understood that compliments from one's pastor are not by themselves to be mistrusted as manipulative. Often, a leader, seeking to give encouragement to an individual, will say something positive to them. Other leaders, because of how they were raised, affirm and compliment people *unconsciously*. Compliments by themselves are not to be mistrusted. It is only a **pattern** of *continual* or *frequent* flattery that suggests manipulation. And that pattern, if it is dangerous, would naturally be accompanied by other exclusivist symptoms.

In light of this discussion on flattery, it is appropriate to note that the apostle Paul affirmed fellow believers without being manipulative. He offered up compliments in his letters which neither drew people's eyes to themselves or to him. Every time he affirmed someone's godliness he did so by thanking *God* – he actually never directly thanked or praised *people*. He would mention a positive behavior of theirs and follow it up with something like, "I thank God for you..." (Rom. 1:8; 1 Cor. 1:4; 2 Cor 9:11,12,15; Eph 1:16; Phil 1:3; Col 1:3; 1 Thes 1:2; 2:13; 3:9; 2 Thes 1:3; 2:13; 2 Tim 1:3; Phile 1:4). With Paul giving that kind of affirmation, people were encouraged in good behavior, but their eyes were drawn back to *God* – not to themselves or to Paul.

Romantic bonds

It is not uncommon in groups led by manipulative charmers, that the charm exuded by a leader appeals to his female followers' romantic or sexual interests. Women from varying exclusivist groups testify that the most painful part of leaving the group was conquering the feeling of having "broken up" with a boyfriend. Although few ever have any sexual contact with their leader, many acknowledge having had a romantic attraction to him. Departing the group tore apart that bond.

Romantic bonds like this are sometimes courted by men in power. They enjoy the loyalty and commitment evoked in their female followers. Many know that if a woman is committed to the group, she can influence her husband to stay as well. Leaders like this continue to pour on the charm with the goal of building the group. They are aware of the power their sex appeal gives them, so they use it. Commonly, these men are also driven by ego – it feels good to be desirable.

It is important to note here, that leaders found to be sexually attractive by women, rarely make blatant passes at them. They are not necessarily men who have plans for adultery or wish for illicit friendships. Chances are that they preach and teach exactly what the Scriptures say about chastity. Outwardly they couldn't be accused of making any directly sexual comments to women. They do however, charm women with their warm and caring manner. Their strength and authority balance well with sensitivity and good listening habits. Many a woman finds in her charming leader all the traits lacking in her husband. Those leaders, who recognize the power that charm gives them, take every opportunity to flirt with their attractive qualities.

This flirting may consist of being firm with husbands from the pulpit regarding their marital responsibilities. Women quietly cheer them on, because they feel so supported, but they also can be tempted to envy the speaker's wife. Marriage counseling offers him further opportunities to win a woman's heart with his understanding and kind, compassionate eyes. No blatant sexual messages are sent, but wooing is going on.

The women who are romantically drawn to their leader may be unaware that their attraction is hormonal in nature. They certainly know they like him, but most, because they want to remain sexually pure, may not *want* to even consider that their affection is inappropriate. Many aren't in-touch with the nature of their feelings until after they leave the group. At that point, when their "bond" is broken, they are able to look back objectively and analyze their behavior. These women will then realize they were caught up in a variety of inappropriate pastimes and imaginations. Some *imagined* their leader was looking at *them* every time he was behind the pulpit. Others looked forward to his hugs each week – the gratification they received proved that the relationship was more than platonic. Some recall going out of their way to compliment him on a sermon. Their romantic interest in the leader was real, but was often too subtle to identify while it was happening.

4. LEADERS CONTROL BY EXERCISING EXCESSIVE AUTHORITY

Common to most exclusivist Christian groups is the exercise of excessive authority by group leaders. These men go far beyond the spiritual authority granted leaders in the Scriptures. Not limiting themselves to matters of church life, faith and morals, they exercise control in people's personal lives.

The Scriptures teach that God uses human leaders to oversee the Body of Christ. He equips them *(Rom 12:8)*, calls them *(Rom 1:1)* and imbues them with the necessary authority *(Heb 13:17)* to shepherd His flock *(Acts 20:28)*. The New Testament used a variety of Greek words to describe these men and their positions of authority:

- *poimen*, **shepherd, pastor** (Eph 4:11)
- *episkopos*, **bishop, overseer, superintendent** (1 Tim 3:1)
- *presbuteros*, **elder, presbyter** (Acts 14:23)
- *didaskalos*, **teacher** (Eph 4:11)
- *hegeomai*, **leader** (Heb 13:7, 17, 24)
- *diakonos*, **deacon** (1 Tim 3:8)
- *prophetes*, **prophet** (Eph 4:11)
- *apostolos*, **apostle** (Eph 4:11)

- *euaggelistes*, **evangelist** (Eph 4:11)
- *leitourgos*, **minister** (Rom 15:16)
- *doulos*, **slave** (1 Cor 9:19)
- *hegeomai* aner, **leading** or **governing men** (Acts 15:22)

The Greek New Testament describes their leadership responsibilities using the following words:
- *proistemi*, **manage, rule over** (Rom 12:8)
- *epimeleomai*, **care for** (1 Tim 3:5)
- *diakonos*, **serve** (Matt 20:26)
- *prosecho*, **watch over, shepherd** (Acts 20:28)
- *bosko*, **feed** (John 21:15)
- *thalpo*, **cherish** (1 Thes 2:7)
- *poimaino*, **tend** (John 21:17)
- *kerusso*, **preach** (2 Tim 4:2)
- *parakaleo*, **instruct, exhort** (1 Thes 4:1)
- *epitimao*, **rebuke** (2 Tim 4:2)
- *oikodome*, **build up, edify** (2 Cor 13:10)
- *elegcho*, **reprove** (2 Tim 4:2)
- *exartizo*, **equip** (2 Tim 3:17)
- *episkopeo*, **willingly oversee** (1 Pet 5:2)
- *paideuo*, **discipline, chasten** (1 Tim 1:20)
- *didaktikos*, **teach** (1 Tim 3:2)
- *noutheteo*, **warn by confrontation** (Acts 20:31)
- *logos*, **account for** (Heb 13:17)

In accepting their spiritual leaders' authority, God's people must not only receive the aforementioned ministries their leaders are responsible to give, but they must also:

- submit to them (Heb 13:17)
- respect them (1 Thes 5:12)
- support them financially (1 Cor 9:11)
- pay close attention to their lives (Heb 13:7)
- imitate their faith (Heb 13:7)

With such a multitude of references to Church leaders and their positions, and with such importance placed by the New Testament on their roles in the shaping and protection of God's flock, it is no surprise that men of authority are tempted to abuse the power of their position. Paul understood this temptation and warned Timothy that elders were to be *mature* believers, lest they fall victim to pride (1 Tim 3:6). The apostle John, in his third epistle, verses 9-10, makes reference to the church leader Diotrephes as one who "loved the preeminence" and fell into the trap of abusing his authority.

The control exercised by exclusivist leaders is often very restrictive and oppressive. Not content with the simple commands and general warnings of Scripture, they set up very specific, extra-biblical rules for conduct. These rules may be written and codified into by-laws and membership agreements, or they may be unspoken, but understood, standards for behavior. Their "shepherding" techniques they staunchly defend as biblical, yet the fact that the rules supplement the Bible reveal their blatant phariseeism. As a sample, these rules typically might dictate:

- how often people must attend meetings

- the need for securing permission to miss meetings
- the length of time members must pray each day
- exactly how they must dress
- how they must wear their hair
- specifically what type of entertainment they may enjoy
- what type of music they may listen to
- what form their education must take
- the manner in which piety and reverence for God is expressed, ie: those who chat in a church sanctuary before a service are judged as unspiritual, etc.

Not only are exclusivist group leaders often very controlling of people's personal lives, but they also exercise intense control over all group decisions and programs, no matter how trivial. Although group leaders may share leadership duties with men outside their clique, and may even assign them titles such as "undershepherd" and "committee head," no real authority is ever released. Those "helpers" are kept on a sort of leash. Group leaders reserve for themselves complete veto power and they frequently use it. Scripture does teach that it is the elders of a local congregation which will be held accountable for that flock, so it is reasonable that they should have veto power over church affairs. However, those leaders who frequently use their veto and continually dictate to everyone exactly how everything must be done are cultivating within their flock some dangerous problems.

Exercising excessive control over people produces in them that same spirit of control. Having been tightly controlled, group members who receive authority immediately become controlling over those under them. They may dominate their committees and study groups and will be reluctant to entrust anyone with responsibility.

It is no surprise that group members, once they have departed these groups and are out from under this type of authority, consistently testify of encountering a feeling of release from "bondage" – a bondage that many claim they were unaware while under it.

5. LEADERS CONTROL BY REQUIRING COMPLETE CONFORMITY OF DOCTRINE

One common trait of many exclusivist groups is the tendency of the leaders to require complete conformity of doctrine among group members. They disallow any questioning of teaching or divergence of thought on any issue or doctrine no matter how trivial. Those members who don't quickly accept group teachings or a leader's answers to questions are perceived as being unsubmissive trouble-makers. Consequently, they are often pressured to leave the group. In some groups they are even excommunicated or "marked".

In an effort to keep the group's members from developing thoughts of their own, group leaders may discourage personal Bible study except with the aid of group-sanctioned study helps and books, or with the oversight of an older brother or sister. They may also forbid or discourage exposure to most outside Christian influences such as radio, TV, tapes, music, books, seminars, or churches.

To discourage members from listening to outside Christian teachers and pastors, leaders may discredit them by continually belittling or making fun of them or their teachings. In the midst of his mocking, a controlling leader may occasionally speak of outside teachers as "deceived" or "misguided," but as was mentioned in a previous section, their mocking attitude demonstrates a lack of Christ-like compassion. A review of Christ's attitude toward holiness and Truth reveals that He never used "sin" to get a laugh. Sin and its deceitfulness was something He hated (Prov 8:13). In fact, for Jesus sin was a matter of life or death. We must trust no Christian leader who professes to lead us to Christ yet lacks His compassion (1 John 4:8).

Isn't unity of the faith important?

The Bible clearly teaches that God values right doctrine and unity of the faith for His people (Eph. 4:11-14; John 17). As shepherds responsible for feeding and overseeing God's sheep Christian leaders must strive to accurately handle the Word of God (2 Tim 2:15; 3:16-17) and use it to equip the saints so that they might find stability through a genuine knowledge of God. It is natural that a shepherd presents Bible Truth to the sheep as accurately as he can, and guards them against false teaching and false Christs (Gal 1:8; 2 Cor 11:4; Acts20:28-31). Jesus said that those who would enter the flock with false doctrine to lead sheep astray (Matt 7:15) are not to be welcomed. They, in fact, are to be avoided and censured (Rom 16:17; 2 John 1:10-11).

Certainly, no shepherd can be faulted for trying to bring a unity of doctrine to the flock he oversees. God is obviously with him in that. In this age of mass publication and open air-waves that job is not an easy one – sheep must be continually warned about dangerous influences. However, there is a limit to the extent a shepherd should control the influences on the flock. A leader exercises his authority excessively when he <u>habitually</u> tries to *control* a believer rather than *warn* him of danger. Intense control of a member's personal life demonstrates a lack of trust in the Holy Spirit (1 John 2:27). A study of the Apostle Paul's *warnings* and *pleadings* to avoid dangerous influences compared with his *commands* to avoid specific ones reveals that he *warned* in general terms more than he *commanded*. Unity of the faith is a high priority with God, but those who "command and forbid" more than they "warn and plead" reveal that they trust more in themselves than in God to control the lives of believers. Typically, such intense control by leaders is just one sign of the blatant phariseeism that pervades the group.

Isn't strong pastoral control biblically warranted?

It is true that Scripture places a high priority upon unity in the faith and submission to spiritual authority, so the exercise of strong pastoral authority seems only right. But, when considered that the Scriptures must be interpreted 2000 years after their writing, a leader goes too far when he makes the basis for fellowship 100% agreement with him on every single issue of doctrine and practice. A respectful tolerance of varying views shows Christian maturity. Without that tolerance pride is given opportunity to grow (Prov 3:7; 26:12; Is 5:21; 1 Cor 8:2).

Doctrines of the historic Christian faith, such as the inspiration of Scripture, the Trinity, the virgin birth, the bodily death and resurrection of the Lord Jesus for the salvation of His people, etc. are essential to the Christian faith, and a leader understandably would require uniform agreement for membership in the flock he oversees. However, when he is intolerant of peripheral doctrinal issues he is "majoring on the minors."

It is important to distinguish here, *holding* a different view from one's pastor and *voicing* to others that view are two different matters. One who *holds* a different view on a peripheral doctrinal issue may simply be a *thinking* individual – one who *speaks* contrary views is *divisive.* It is imperative for anyone under authority to support their leaders with an attitude of submission and respect (Heb 13:17; 1 Thes 5:12). They therefore must not sow seeds of discontent or mistrust by letting other group members know their disagreements with their shepherds. Like all matters of a sensitive nature, they should be spoken about only with those they involve (Prov 17:9; 11:9,13; 20:19; 26:20; Ps 101:5; Lev 19:16). Whether the views expressed by a dissenting sheep are heretical or not, it is appropriate for leaders to ask to leave those who refuse to respect their authority and those who voice their disagreements behind their back (Rom 16:17; Tit. 3:10). Divisiveness simply cannot be tolerated. Those leaders, however, who demand perfect agreement in every trivial doctrinal issue strive for unreasonable control and contribute to the group's exclusiveness.

* * * * * * * * * * * * * * * *

FOR THOSE WHO HAVE LEFT AN EXCLUSIVIST
GROUP ...

HEALING THE HURT OF ABUSE
Dealing with Bitterness, Anger and Blame

It is not uncommon that those who leave exclusivist groups depart with a great sense of disillusionment. The ones they once implicitly trusted, they now doubt. The leaders they once admired, they now view with suspicion. While in the group they had a great sense of security and confidence, but after leaving they find themselves feeling alone and confused.

Close friends who remain in the group now avoid them or act awkward when in their presence. Leaders, who used to love them, now warn others about them, even portraying them as dangerous. The very group they gave their lives to, they now find has rejected them. Many feel used and abused. The emotional pain for some is overwhelming.

Hasty reactions

Many who leave an exclusivist group, feel so hurt that they intensely want to rescue their loved ones still there. Some try to help the group dissolve by doing mass mailings which warn remaining members of their plight. Others speak out in an effort to caution outsiders about the group's failings. Such passion is understandable.

Despite the natural inclination to rescue loved ones from what they see as danger, ex-exclusivists must not react too quickly. They must be careful of their zeal, because motives are often not pure in one nursing fresh wounds from rejection. All too commonly, it is not *love* which drives us to influence the old group, but frustration fueled by anger. Yes, it is appropriate to hate the devil for the deception he has wrought, but when we our wounds are fresh, the line between hating the devil and resenting those he has deceived can be a muddy one.

Fresh anger is poison to the Christian and can easily pollute any efforts to offer genuine spiritual help. James tells us that "… *the wrath of man does not accomplish the righteousness of God (Jam 1:20)*. It is usually best that ex-members work through any unforgiveness and bitterness, and before they attempt to rescue all those endangered by the group.

The reason for this caution is because many ex-exclusivists are completely unaware that they are bitter. They believe they are simply "hurt," and in an effort to do good, they inadvertently sow seeds of chaos and confusion, hurting the faith of many sincere believers in the process. It is, therefore, of the utmost importance that ex-exclusivists deal first with their motives before acting on their zeal.

Victims or Perpetrators?

It is not uncommon that upon leaving a group, ex-members begin to feel like they have been victims of some kind of "spiritual abuse." They are angry with those who intimidated them into giving their lives to the group, and then rejected them. Not surprisingly, in recent years much has been written to address this anger and confusion. Books on exclusive churches, "victimization," and "spiritual abuse" are now easy to find in Christian bookstores.

These books have identified a very real problem. However, most of them share one serious flaw. They suggest that those who leave exclusivist groups are "victims" of others. To consider oneself a victim is a great *hindrance* to quick recovery – not an *aid*. This is because a true "victim" is one who is a passive recipient of some harm – not one who contributed. Those who believe themselves to be innocent victims avoid seeing their responsibility, and therefore cannot properly deal with the part they contributed to their deception. Ultimately, a victim mentality allows us to blame others for our responses to them.

Nothing in Scripture suggests that God will excuse those who were drawn into deception. Not one of the seven churches in Revelations who had been deceived by the devil was excused by Christ. Paul did not speak to the Galatian church as if they were blameless victims of false doctrine. In fact, he told Timothy the opposite – it is our flesh that attracts us to those who would tickle our ears.

*2 Tim 4:3 For the time will come when they will not endure sound doctrine; but **wanting to have their ears tickled**, they will accumulate for themselves teachers in accordance to their own desires;*

Yes, God holds false teachers responsible for their deception. And yes, they will answer for stumbling others (Luke 17:1), but nothing in Scripture suggests that those deceived are innocent and excused from holding false doctrines or being proud of their associations. The bottom line is that most people, who are drawn to exclusivist groups, are drawn not by their *new nature*, but by their *flesh*. As this booklet has sought to demonstrate, the exclusivism that sets such a group apart and holds it together is rooted in pride, and group leaders only have power in people's lives, because they appeal to people's sinful pride and a desire to be special.

If we want to be free from the effects of an exclusivist group, we must get free from our pride. It drew us to the group and kept us there. We are not *victims*, but *co-perpetrators*. For us to be "healed" we must stop seeing ourselves as innocent victims. We must not justify our anger at our old leaders. We will lack wholeness as long as we continue to blame others. Our old leaders will be held responsible by God for their ungodliness and improper leadership, but not for their followers' responses to them.

Remember, in all such groups leaders are proud, but so are the members. Group leaders may be oppressive, but members only follow because they give the leaders power to control them. Generally, if someone has power to intimidate us, it is only because we gave it to him.

Our experience has been that "victims" never seem to get over their experience, so repeatedly talk about their experiences with others who have left the group. They rehearse the failings of their leaders and the causes for the offense over and over. Yes, it is true, that when humans experience great trauma they tend to talk about it over and over, but many never recover from a loss if they keep the memories of that trauma fresh and alive. In fact, when the trauma is rooted in a group we have left, it is often a sign of misplaced blame and abiding bitterness.

Resolving the Hurt and Anger

The Bible warns us clearly that when we hold onto "hurt" it is nothing more than nurturing anger. Staying angry is one of the most destructive things a Christian can do. Ephesians 4:26-27 makes this very clear: *"In your anger do not sin": Do not let the sun go down while you are still angry,* **and do not give the devil a foothold.** Verse 27 indicates that it is critical that we resolve our anger, because if we do not, then we literally give Satan influence in our life.

Holding on to anger does give the devil sway in our lives. Yes, even we as believers, indwelt by the Holy Spirit, are warned that Satan can influence us. And if Satan can capitalize on our anger and cause great turmoil through the exposure of an exclusivist group, then he will do it. It is therefore critical that we identify all unforgiveness on our part.

How can we determine if we are nurturing unforgiveness in our life?

In the fourth chapter of Ephesians, verse 31, Paul lists five expressions of unforgiveness. He tells us

69

"Get rid of all bitterness, rage and anger, brawling and slander, along with every form of malice." These expressions of unforgiveness are defined as follows:

BITTERNESS: *pikria;* polluted, contaminated, sour, smelly

When anger is left unresolved it, turns to bitterness, *completely* infecting our spirit and outlook on life. It ultimately hardens our heart.

RAGE: *thumos;* wrathful outbursts, impassioned agitated *feelings;* anger in its first-stage

If left unchecked, our initial feeling of inner indignation will produce an abiding and active anger.

ANGER: *orge;* fierce passion

While *rage* is more indicative of an *inward* impassioned *response, anger* suggests an abiding condition of the mind, often with a view to vengeance.

BRAWLING: *krauge;* noisy, like a raven's cry

Those ruled by their rage can be tempted to clamorous arguments and fights.

SLANDER: *blasphemia;* to blaspheme, revile, rail

The natural fruit of bitterness is to verbally attack the object of our anger, either confrontationally or by gossip.

Symptoms of Unforgiveness

- constant irritability, always snaps, easily angered, competitive

- nit-picking, critical, faultfinding
- rudeness, constant sarcastic cuts and digs
- over-willingness to complain about shortcomings to others
- dwelling on the offense, reliving the cause of "injury"
- impatience, intolerance
- rejoicing when the other is humbled
- saying hurtful things to them – embarrasses – degrades
- harping on past failures
- vengeful, wants to hurt back
- hateful, demeaning, scornful thoughts

We cannot repent of bitterness until we forgive. We cannot forgive as long as we:

- hold on to anger
- justify, minimize, or excuse our resentment
- blame others for our responses to them
- allow fear to control us
- ignore God's sovereign hand

The most subtle symptom of bitterness

The primary, but least obvious symptom of bitterness is the tendency to judge the *heart* of the one who has hurt us. When we are bitter at someone, we tend to decide we know their heart and their true motives in *anything*. Because we won't trust them, *all* their motives become suspect. We may not be aware of any residual anger, but if we perceive the offender as being completely and thoroughly evil, then we can know for certain that we are bitter, and our hearts are dangerously on their way to becoming hard.

In 1 Corinthians 4:5 **God** makes it clear that only He has the ability to accurately know human motives and is therefore the only One who can judge the heart.

> *"Therefore judge nothing before the appointed time; wait till the Lord comes. He will bring to light what is hidden in darkness and will expose the motives of men's hearts. At that time each will receive his praise from God."* (See also Jer.11:20 & Rev.2:23)

It is only God who is capable of accurately knowing the motives and intentions of people. Yes, people can be evil through and through, but only *God* can know that of a person, not *us*. As soon as we believe we have the power to judge another's heart we have stepped into God's role, and have opened the door to our own spiritual demise.

Inevitably, some at this point, will resist accepting that their judgment of their ex-leader's heart is a sign of bitterness. They are so confident of their assessment of his motives, and are so consumed with what seems to them as justifiable anger, that they can't even begin to consider the possibility that they could be wrong in their assessment. The same attitude of pride and judgment they received from *him* now rules them and colors their perception of him. How tragic!

Is someone else responsible for our responses to them?

When we are offended by someone it is natural for us to justify our anger toward them. And when we hold an offense against another, we easily believe the worst of them. However, we cannot blame others for our reactions to them. The anger with which we react is not their fault.

We may have been manipulated by our leader, but we must not forget that it was us who gave him the power to intimidate and control us. Our desire for his approval is what empowered him to "hurt" us. If, in our insecurity, we hadn't sought his approval, he couldn't have influenced us. Since it was we who gave the leader the power to hurt us, it is only ourselves we can blame.

Consider the fact that many people visited, but did not return to the group. They were not controlled by the leader – they did not want his approval – they did not perceive him as needed for the sake of their self esteem.

Consider the following testimony of one such anonymous ex-member:

For a year of my life I was in pain from what I thought was spiritual abuse. That year followed my departure from a fellowship with which I had been involved for more than 10 years. My pastor during that time had been very intimidating to me. My fear of him and what he thought of me had ruled my life. After leaving and getting out from under his "power," I looked back and blamed him for the way I thought he "made" me feel. The reason I was sure it was **his** problem and not **mine** was that I had watched others be intimidated by him for many years. After seeing what he did to them I was confident I was not alone. I was sure he was an egomaniac on a "power trip," one who was using the people of God to build his own little empire.

After I left the church I found myself hurt and angry, because of the way I thought **he** made me feel. It wasn't until 2 years later that I realized that he wasn't responsible for the way I reacted to his strong personality. He was not **making** me feel any certain way. **He was not responsible for my responses to him – I was.** Until then I had been blaming him for that which I was responsible. Certainly, on Judgment Day he will give account for how he treated people and for whether or not he acted in a godly fashion, but he will not be held accountable for the responses of those who allowed themselves to be intimidated by him. Each of them will be responsible for their own behavior. It was their choice to stay under his authority, and it was they who gave him the power to approve or disapprove of them. (name withheld)

How many of us blame those who intimidate us for how *we* respond to their intimidation? Because of what we think is our "condition," we believe ourselves incapable of loving them. As long as we exempt ourselves from our responsibilities to love those who have made themselves our "enemies," we will remain immobilized. We will be *crippled*, but not by what we call "emotional pain," but by *bitterness!* Once infected with bitterness, not only do we give the devil a foothold in our life, but long after we have left the exclusivist group we will still be ruled by the leader we so despised. While we were in the group it was our need for his approval that ruled us – now that we are out, it is our resentment towards him that overshadows us. May all those who read this identify their bitterness and be free from it once and for all.

God's solution for unforgiveness is not very complicated. Ephesians 4:32 directs us, *"Be kind and compassionate to one another,* **forgiving each other, just as in Christ God forgave you.***"* Colossians 3:13 affirms the same message, *"Bear with each other and forgive whatever grievances you may have against one another.* **Forgive as the Lord forgave you.***"* These commands directly compare our forgiveness of others to God's forgiveness of us – *both are completely undeserved.*

This type of mercy presumes the offender is never worthy of forgiveness. But then again, that is the very nature of mercy – it implies that the offender deserves justice. Mercy is justice-withheld. Paul points out that the way we conquer bitterness and find mercy for others is to get a fresh dose of mercy ourselves. He directs us to look back to our own unworthiness before God, realizing that we were nothing more than God's enemy (Rom 5:10), and that we deserved only judgment in Hell when God decided to cancel our debt.

A great sense of self-importance (pride) is at the root of bitterness. If we can renew our own sense of indebtedness and humility before God we will be able to express that same mercy to others. We must not believe the lie that *our* situation is different. God has declared the simple solution – the power to forgive is found first by admitting our bitterness and the pride from which it stems, and then canceling the offender's debt in the same way ours was canceled by God when we didn't deserve it. It is through our humility before God that we will find the grace we need to forgive (James 4:6-10).

* * * * * * * * * * * * * * *

HOW TO IDENTIFY EXCLUSIVISM IN A GROUP OR SPIRITUAL LEADER

The following list of symptoms summarizes what has been discussed in this book. Each symptom by itself is not necessarily indicative of such an exclusive group, but all taken together they strongly suggest imbalance and danger.

1. The group will present itself as serious about personal holiness, so will appeal to earnest Christians who intensely want to be holy
   - Their standards for personal holiness will be very conservative and challenging
   - Their sobering sounding tape titles, article headlines, and exposés attract serious-minded believers
   - Their emphasis on how they are more "on fire" than the "lukewarm" church will attract those who agree that the modern church is weak

2. The group communicates that only *they* are enlightened and have the Truth, or at the least, are one of a few who are on the cutting edge of what God is doing in the world today
   - Leaders as well as group members dwell on those things that make them unique and set apart from the rest of the body of Christ

- They seem to look for things in which to take pride, ie: their knowledge of the true biblical standard, their use of the only acceptable Bible translation, their proper recognition of biblical customs, etc.
- Group members frequently discuss the shortcomings of those they consider unenlightened. Some may mock, but others will couch their criticism in compassionate sounding expressions of concern
- Their elevated view of themselves may cause them to doubt that few, if any, outsiders are truly saved

3. Their dominant theme is often criticism and exposure of "false teachers" *(Excluding organizations that are purposed in ministering to cults.)*
- They have a judgmental, faultfinding style of teaching, which may be characterized by uncompassionate mocking, scorning, and belittling of those they regard as "spiritually blind"
    Prov 21:24 The proud and arrogant man — "Mocker" is his name; he behaves with overweening pride.
    Prov 11:12 "He who belittles his neighbor lacks sense."
- Leaders' constant criticism of others will eliminate all outside leaders as respectable, effectively pointing followers back to them as the only leaders worth following
- They may label as "false teachers" all who do not agree with their interpretations of the Bible, which often, will be everyone outside the group. Not

uncommonly, they will publicly list the names of highly prominent evangelical leaders whom they regard as false teachers.

4. The tone of their writings and teaching will reflect a judgmental, condescending arrogance
- Their general attitude may be hostile and angry, which they will justify, labeling it as righteous anger
- The arrogant, judgmental spirit of their ministry will often quickly infect those who drink from their well
- Newcomers, once infected, will discover that they are suspicious and hypercritical of the spiritual leaders they have trusted and respected in the past

5. They claim to offer new "light," presenting their ideas as more insightful than all others
- Their ideas are non-traditional, and they may claim to be restoring lost elements of the gospel
- Leaders frequently emphasize their enlightenment, authority, or whatever else gives them credibility, to attract and keep followers. (They trust in their fleshly efforts, and do not trust that biblical revelation stands on its own authority, or that the Holy Spirit will be faithful to bear witness to the Truth)
- Their emphasis on new "insights" will leave newcomers feeling a sense of excitement at having their eyes opened
- Doctrines or practices considered by most to be minor, they will deem absolutely critical, and they

will then condemn or belittle all those who do not elevate or hold to the same doctrines or practices

6. They are preoccupied with what they believe are the only acceptable ways to show honor and respect for God (Mat 23:23-28)
- Place great emphasis on issues related to the outward expressions of respect for God, ie: they are absorbed with proper or improper days of worship, avoiding christianized pagan holidays and customs, appropriate attitudes of sobriety and reverence in worship, correct expressions of the fear of God, etc.
- They reverence the *things* of God more than the character of God. That is, they are more likely to judge others according to the group's standards of symbolic respect, than on the basis of whether or not they manifest the love and humility of Christ.
- They claim to be honoring God better than others, and seem unaware that their pride and judgmental attitude negate all their outward righteousness.

7. They will tend toward Phariseeism (John 7:24)
- Preoccupied with outward "appearance" of holiness, so great emphasis is placed upon cleaning up the outside, ie: grooming, makeup, hairstyles, clothes, jewelry, etc.

- Tend to define holiness more as the avoidance of carnal influences, rather than the presence of the love and character of Christ.

- They are not content with the general standards God created in Scripture, but create extra-biblical rules, which in their opinion, are proper applications of Scripture for everyone.

- Hold others accountable to their personal, extra-biblical standards of holiness, ie: they have well-defined rules related to TV watching, music, entertainment, education, parenting, possessions, etc. (God anticipates that we will extrapolate from Scripture personal rules for ourselves and our families, but when we judge others by those personal standards we enter into Phariseeism.)

8. Leaders will exercise strong control over group members

- Membership in the group requires adherence to many extra-biblical rules and standards.

- Once members, people are intimidated into submission by group leaders. Fear of consequences keeps members in line.

- If asked about those who have left the group, rarely will leaders speak of an ex-member with respect. Leaders will typically portray all or most ex-members as blind, deceived, or rebellious. Ex-members, in fact, are often castigated as infectious, and are subjected to shunning by the group.

As you consider the things you have read here, please remember that a group is not dangerous because its members are on fire for Jesus and take seriously their calling to live holy lives. That is actually the calling of the Church. No, it not intensity that makes a group dangerous. It is the presence of pride. This elevated self-view will not be obvious to group members. They will know too well that only God is to receive glory for whatever good is in their lives, so they will not overtly give credit to themselves. However, they will glory in feelings of specialness, their pride expressing itself in condescension and arrogant judgment. They will not realize that it is an exalted view of their own insights that makes them quick to discredit all others. May the Lord protect His sheep from those wolves that creep in to devour them. Amen!

Made in the USA
Columbia, SC
13 August 2020

16296962R00046